Oldway Mansion

Historic home of the Singer family

First published 2009 Torbay books
Copyright © Paul Hawthorne

Torbay Books
7 Torquay Road
Paignton
Devon
TQ3 3DU

ISBN 978-0-9551857-6-2

Printed and bound in Great Britain by
Newton Print, Newton Abbot.

DEDICATION

"I was delighted to be invited to write the foreword for this hugely interesting booklet - compiled by Paul Hawthorne.

Oldway is very close to my heart. My mother Winnaretta was born a Singer and I lived in 'Big Oldway' as we called it with my parents and brother George for five years until we moved into 'Little Oldway' in 1935. However, I and my brother still managed to spend a lot of time exploring the gardens and playing hide-and-seek in the house, no doubt much to the chagrin of the members of the Torbay Country Club!

This booklet is a fascinating account in pictures of all the different ativities at Oldway over the years. In 2007, I held a large gathering of the decendants of Isaac Singer at Oldway. At that time, the 'Friends of Oldway' was formed with Paul Hawthorne as Chairman. I and all my family are all very supportive of this endeavour and heartily recommend this booklet."

Rhodanthe Winnaretta Selous
(Patron of the friends of Oldway)

Right Isaac Merrit Singer
by Edward Harrison May
Oil on cavas 1869

National Portrait Gallery,
Smithsonian Institution;
gift of the Singer
Company

ISAAC SINGER AND THE SEWING MACHINE

Isaac Merritt Singer had patented his Singer Sewing Machine in 1851, at the age of 41. By the time he came to England in 1870 he was already one of the richest men alive, and, to quote newspapers of the time, had become a "household word". He considered himself the "original inventor and patentee of the first practical sewing machine". He had not actually invented the sewing machine, but refined and improved on the existing ones available to create his unique Singer model.

The combination of Isaac's flair for invention, combined with his partner Mr Clark's business skill, sold the machines in their millions. Clark pioneered various sales techniques to ensure their success. He introduced hire-purchase, allowing people to purchase Singer machines for five dollars per month rather than paying the full price outright. Beautiful women were paid to work on machines in shop windows in busy high streets, and interested crowds gathered around to watch them. Many husbands were uncomfortable with the idea of paying for a machine that did a job their wives did for free, and the machines saved women so much time that they were free to devote their energies to education and self-improvement. To establish the Singer sewing machine's

respectability and to reassure society at large, free machines were given to the wives of clergymen. Sewing machines became an essential part of the modern home.

Above Singer no.1 - the original lock-stitch machine, nicknamed "Jenny Lind" after a famous Swedish singer.

Scandal in his personal life had forced Isaac to leave his life in America. By the time he left for Europe in 1862, he had had eighteen children by several different women. His partner Clark felt this was not helping the Singer company sell to the conservative middle classes. His new French wife, Isabelle Boyer, was thirty years his junior, and together they settled in Paris and raised another six children. Their comfortable life was rudely interrupted, however, by the war between France and Prussia in 1870.

As the Prussian army reached the outskirts of Paris, Isaac Singer and his young wife and family finally decided to flee to London. They went by train. The danger of sabotage was such that a man had to walk in front of the train to check none of the rails had been destroyed or removed. The youngest of their family of six, Franklin Morse, was just months old. The year was 1870.

The family transferred to London, moving into a large town house minutes from Buckingham Palace. Isaac by now was not well, and his worsening health soon forced the family to move on once again. His doctor advised him to spend the winter in Torquay, already famous for its mild climate. And so it was that one of the world's richest men took his wife and young family down to the remote west of England with the intention of finding a house to rent for six months before returning to London to continue their lives. They arrived in Torquay in February 1872.

One would expect the arrival of one of the world's richest men in a small Devon seaside town to cause quite a stir; Isaac and his family arrived almost unnoticed. Rather than stay at the new Imperial Hotel, where royalty were often guests, Isaac chose to stay at the more modest Victoria and Albert Hotel. It seems the family wanted to keep a low profile, away from public attention. The very week they arrived the local paper, the Torquay Directory, listed a small eight-acre estate for sale, slightly apart from the bustle of Torquay society, just to the north of the emerging village of Paignton. Whilst at the hotel Isaac met the young architect George Soudon Bridgman. Bridgman knew Paignton well, and had great plans for the town. He also knew the area that was to become the Oldway Estate, and would have recommended it strongly to Isaac as a place to rest and gather his strength. That Paignton was just starting to develop would have been a great attraction to Isaac – he would be able to nurture it and shape its development. It would also offer the peace and quiet he needed to regain his health.

Paignton had remained unchanged for hundreds of years. It was a sleepy village set back from the sea around its medieval church, and famous for the blossom of its

apple trees and its sweet cabbages. The railway had arrived in 1859, but even that had yet to cause any great change, and life for the village continued very much as it had done before. Isaac's arrival in Paignton was to herald a new era for the town, and mark the beginning of a unique relationship between his family and the local people that would continue through generations.

Opposite Isabelle and children in Paris in 1868. From left to right: Winnaretta, an infant Paris, Washington (seated) and Mortimer.

Above Paignton when Isaac arrived was a village just beginning to develop into a resort.

LITTLE OLDWAY

In May 1872 Isaac, his young wife Isabelle, and their six children – Mortimer, Washington, Winnaretta, Paris, Belle Blanche and Franklin, all squeezed into the pleasant villa of (Little) Oldway. This was a charming but very modest house for a man of his wealth. Oldway Villa had been built around 1850.

It was taken on a six month let, and Isaac's London house was kept fully staffed and awaiting his return. It was then that something quite unexpected happened. Isaac fell in love with his life in Devon – in particular with the town and the people of Paignton and so decided to make this his permanent home. Two things were missing to make his life complete: a bigger estate and a new, modern residence. He set about buying all the adjoining land he could and commissioned Bridgman to assist him in the design of his dream home. A proud American with a large family should, Isaac said, live in a wigwam, and this is what Bridgman was instructed to design for him. And Isaac insisted it was to be a big wigwam at that.

Right The Singers installed at Little Oldway circa 1872.

Above right Paignton Pier, designed by Bridgman for Arthur Hyde Dendy.

Below right Bridgman in Masonic dress.

MR GEORGE SOUDON BRIDGMAN

The 31-year-old George Soudon Bridgman had recently designed the new Torbay Hotel on Torquay seafront. Isaac's London home was in a similar French style, and this, combined with Bridgman's youth, made Isaac select him rather than an older, more famous architect. As Bridgman would discover however, Isaac didn't so much want an architect as a draftsman– someone to adopt and map out his own personal ideas for the builders to follow. As an inventor and engineer Isaac wanted to design and choose everything from the shape of the house to the location of doors and fireplaces, and even the type of hinges used. This was to be Isaac's ultimate dream house – everything he had ever wanted was to be included. It would feature the latest in central heating systems from America (Isaac felt the cold very badly indeed and warmth was a top priority for him). Isaac had been inspired by his time in Paris, and sent Bridgman to France (now that the war was over) to study his special requirements for his new house at source.

The crowning glory of the Wigwam was to be a fully working theatre on the ground floor – the work of a very young Frank Matcham, who would go on to become one of the greatest theatre designers in

the country. Isaac had been in love with the theatre since he was young, and at one point had even toured America with his own company of actors "The Merritt Players", using money made from an earlier invention. Now he would have his own stage to perform on.

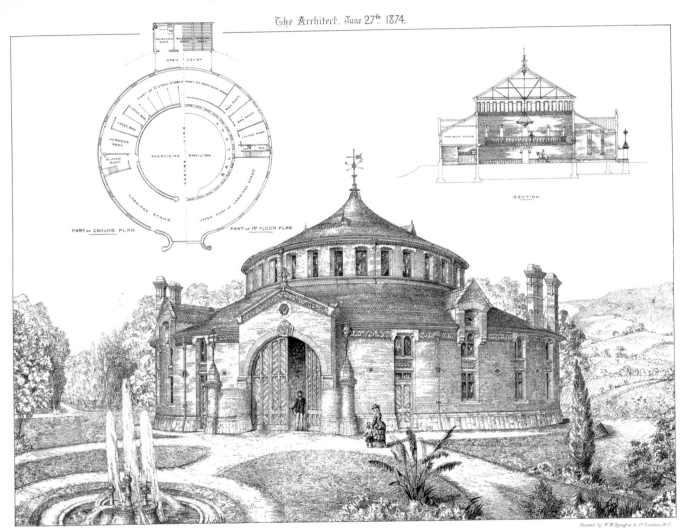

The Architect, June 27th 1874

STABLING & EXERCISING PAVILION, PAIGNTON, TORQUAY.
GEO. SOUDON BRIDGMAN, ARCHITECT.

Mrs Isabelle Singer laid the corner stone of the new house in May 1873, but by that time another part of the estate was already well under way. Isaac had a love of public entertaining, and in particular of giving children's parties. His health had recovered, but in his own words, "although he looked strong, he was not so" – he knew he was nearing the end of his life. Despite this he instructed Bridgman to start the Arena (which is known today as the Rotunda) before his Wigwam. By day, this was to be a centre for exercise and horse-riding; by night, with its polished wooden floor in place, it was an ideal venue for entertainment and dancing. It was completed by the end of 1873.

On New Year's Day 1874 the children of Paignton were invited inside the great double doors of the new building. They were greeted by the tremendous sight of a 26 ft. Christmas tree decked with over a thousand presents. "A Merry Christmas and a Happy New Year to one and all" was spelt out in flowers and evergreens adorning the front of the balcony. An excellent lunch was laid for everyone in the carriage stand space to the left and right inside of the entrance, with the Rhine Band giving musical accompaniment. All the presents on the tree were numbered, and four numbers given to each child to claim their prizes. There were "all prizes and no blanks", observed the local paper. Dancing followed, and Mr Singer entertained with a dinner party at his house in the evening.

Mr James Matcham, a Plymouth building contractor, was commissioned to build the Mansion and Rotunda, and employed a workforce of 140 men to do so. Mr Singer paid his workmen well, to such an extent that employers in Paignton complained at the time of how he was forcing local wages up. On the day of the laying of the corner stone a dinner was held for the workforce in the local Assembly Rooms at Mr Singer's expense, which was very well received. With good wages came strict conditions, however. At this very dinner Mr Bridgman made it clear in a short speech to the men that if there was ever a strike of any kind the construction of the house would be abandoned indefinitely.

Isaac's wish to be at the centre of his project did not stop once the plans had been finalized. Living only 100 metres away from the construction site allowed him to keep a close eye on the project's progress; doubtless Isabelle might have preferred to live further

Opposite The Rotunda, as it appeared in The Architect June 27th 1874.

Next page The Wigwam from The Architect June 27th 1874.

away from such a large building site. Mr Matcham too would have to be patient when his patron chose to intervene: "often when a portion had not been built according to his own idea, and did not please him, he would have it taken down and rebuilt after another plan", commented the local press.

Isaac's talent for self-publicity ensured that drawings of his new Wigwam and Rotunda were printed for a national audience in The Architect in June 1874. The entrance front of the house pictured showed the French inspiration of the design, in contrast to the dominant Italianate style of building in the area.

The article said the new house was to be finished in the autumn of that year, but in reality it was not to be completed until well into the summer of 1875. The entrance front used Portland stone, with columns of Aberdeen granite for the entrance porch. A long, sloping carriage ramp took arriving guests up to the main entrance, which was on today's first floor. The Singer monogram was proudly displayed on the large chimney flue on the right. A fountain lay between the Wigwam and the Rotunda. At the time the house was built, many of the rooms would have had panoramic sea views; today these views are obscured by trees from all but the second and third floors.

LIBRARY SCHOOL ROOM WAITING ROOM

OPEN TO BASEMENT

CARRIAGE

SLOPE

GROUND FLOOR

BUILDING A WIGWAM

The entire house was faced with Jenning's cream- coloured terracotta bricks, and used over 6,000 ft of glass. A carving of a native American chief firing a bow and arrow on top of a flag pole finished off the whole design (his son Paris was later to donate this to the town, and it stood for many years on the seafront at Paignton on top of the bandstand).

As the newly completed house was being decorated in July 1875, Isaac's health worsened and he died. Finishing the Rotunda first had meant he had never enjoyed living in the house he had spent much effort and energy designing.

His last years spent at Paignton were doubtless some of the happiest of his life. His popularity and behind-the-scenes generosity are best described by those who knew him at the time:

"at some seasons of the year he regularly gave dinners or teas to the people, and bountifully distributed food with a secret hand to those he knew to be in need. Being possessed of a princely income he used it, somewhat unlike some of our wealthy nobles, for the good of those around him, and for those who needed assistance."

Torquay Times, July 1875

"We ne'er shall look on his like again."

W. J. McCormack, trusted steward of the Singer family

Left The Wigwam from the southwest. The west front remains largely unchanged today. Bridgman had been sent to France by Isaac to study details such as the ironwork he wanted at source.

OLDWAY HOUSE, PAIGNTON.

Anniversary of

MR. ISAAC M. SINGER'S BIRTHDAY,

OCTOBER 27TH, 1873.

PROGRAMME.

SCENE FROM HENRY VIII. .. .. "Cardinal Wolsey and Cromwell."
MASTER MORTIMER SINGER.

SOLO .. .. "Spooning on the Sands."
MISS WINARETTA E. SINGER.

SOLO .. .. "Courting in the Rain."
MASTER MORTIMER SINGER.

"BREAKING THE SPELL."

A COMIC OPERA IN ONE ACT.

Characters.

JENNY WOOD .. (Maid of the "Rising Sun" Tavern)
MISS ALICE M. SINGER.

OLD MATTHEW .. ..(A Chelsea Pensioner).. MR. M. G. RICE.

PETER BLOOM .. .. (Gardner) MR. JOHN CUSHWAY.

PIANOFORTE BY MISS FLORENCE MATCHAM.

Scene.

Garden adjoining a Tavern.

I. M. SINGER.
Sewing Machine.

3 Sheets—Sheet 1.

No. 61,270.   Patented Jan'y 15, 1867.

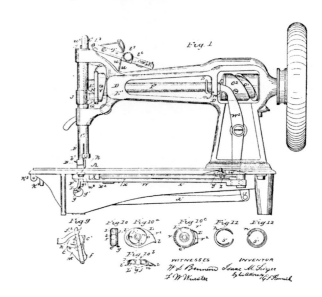

Above Left The family
take to the stage to
celebrate Isaac's birthday.

Above Right Original
patent drawing of an
early Singer round bobbin
sewing machine, 1867.

Left Isaac Singer during his time in Paignton.

THE FUNERAL

Isaac had commissioned a great family tomb, but his wish to be buried in his beloved Paignton could not be met – Paignton had no cemetery at this time, so the closest practical option was Torquay. The death of Isaac Merritt Singer led to a phenomenal outpouring of grief in the local towns. Thousands turned out to pay their respects at his funeral, shops and offices closed for the day, and people lined the streets to watch the funeral procession. The cortège was made up of eighty carriages – and was so long that as the first ones arrived at the cemetery at Hele in Torquay, the last ones were just passing the cliffs at Livermead on the seafront.

A solemn period of mourning was soon broken by great international scandal. Isaac died one of the richest men alive, with a fortune of over $13,000,000. Coming to Paignton had allowed him to put his notorious life in America behind him, but now it was to catch up abruptly with Isabelle Singer and their young family.

All of Isaac's recognised children – twenty-four in all – were left money in his will, leaving every one of them very comfortably off. Their mothers, with the exception of Isabelle, did not fare so well, however, and this was to cause problems in one case in particular.

In America, Mary Ann Sponsler filed a law suit claiming she, and not Isabelle, was the rightful Mrs Singer, and she should inherit his vast wealth. A huge scandal followed, as all the intimate details of Miss Sponsler's many years with Isaac were splashed across the front pages of the world's press.

It was true that she had been Isaac's loyal companion from when he was penniless to when he became wealthy, and together

they had had several children. Her claim to be the rightful Mrs Singer fell down, however, on two counts. Firstly they had never married. Isaac was married when they first met, and when he was subsequently divorced and free to marry her, he had absolutely refused to do so; this led to their eventual separation. Secondly, she herself had later married. In January 1876, after six months in which every painful detail of Isaac's earlier life had been shared with the world's newspaper reading public, the judge declared Isabelle to be Isaac's lawful wedded wife after all, to everyone in Paignton's great relief.

Upon Isaac's death his great wealth went into a trust as his will instructed – controlled by his New York lawyer Mr Hawley and his local Paignton physician, Dr Pridham. The two were charged specifically with completing the house and gardens exactly as Isaac had intended "at considerable expense".

Oposite The Singer Tomb in Torquay cemetery.

Above The Wigwam from the soth east. Behind the stepped east front was Isaac's theatre.

LIFE WITHOUT ISAAC

Although shaken by the publicity of the trial, Isabelle continued to live at the Wigwam for another four years.

She continued Isaac's charitable tradition, hosting fund-raising events in the Rotunda for local good causes. The Singer Trustees constructed the first part of the sea wall at Preston, protecting the land that lay behind.

Towards 1879, however, it seems the time had come for the family to move on from Paignton. Isabelle was concerned about the children being able to marry well whilst in Devon, and decided to relocate to Paris. Isaac's will ensured that, should she remarry, she would be obliged to give up living in his dream home. When, as the newly married Vicomtesse D'Estenburgh, she returned to Paignton in January 1879, she knew she could not stay long. It is around this time in Paris that Isabelle Singer is believed to have been a model for the Statue of Liberty by the sculptor Bartholdi.

Not all the family would move to Paris, however. Mortimer, the eldest of the children, could not bring himself to leave at all; such was his fondness for Paignton.

On the night the carriage came to take the family away to the station, he stowed away in the local postman's cart and escaped. Whilst the family were making a fresh start in Paris, Mortimer, already 16 years old, was setting up home with his newly adopted Paignton family, the Eastleys. Mr Eastley had been the trusted lawyer and friend of Isaac. He had "adopted" Mortimer, but subsequently Mortimer and his brothers would adopt them all as an integral part of their extended family.

Above The Wigwam seen from the west, with its extensive conservatories and the sweeping carriage ramp that took you up to the entrance on the first floor.

Above Steartfield House, home of Washington Singer.

Right Lillie Singer, married to Paris Singer in 1887 in Hobart, Tasmania.

FRIENDS OF

OLDWAY

Membership Application

PLEASE PRINT ONLY ONE NAME PER APPLICATION

Title: .... First Name ....

Surname ....

Address ....

....

.... Post code ....

Telephone ....

Email ....

I enclose my subscription/donation of (£1.00 minimum)

£ ....

that from this date ....
confirms my membership of 'Friends of Oldway'.
I understand that receipt of my subscription/donation
will be confirmed by receipt of the next mailing.
If a specific receipt is required please send s.a.e. to:
Honorary Secretary, Friends of Oldway,
c/o The Devon School of English, 1 Lower Polsham Road,
Paignton, Devon TQ3 2AF

DATA PROTECTION ACT 1998 Members' data will be used for administrating
Friends of Oldway activities/mailing only.

Signature ....

PLEASE SEE ATTACHED GIFT AID DECLARATION

Gift Aid Declaration

PLEASE PRINT ONLY ONE NAME PER DECLARATION

If you are a UK Taxpayer please fill in
the attached form which will enable Friends of Oldway
to claim an additional 28p in each £1 from
the Government to boost our finances,
at no extra cost to yourself.

Detail of Donor:

Title: .... First Name ....

Surname ....

Address ....

....

.... Post code ....

I would like Friends of Oldway to treat all donations
that I have made since 7 December 2007, and
all future donations as Gift Aid donations,
unless I notify you otherwise.

Please tick one of these boxes:

☐ I am a UK Taxpayer

☐ I am not a UK Taxpayer

Signature ....

Please return the completed form to:
Honorary Secretary, Friends of Oldway,
c/o The Devon School of English, 1 Lower Polsham Road,
Paignton, Devon TQ3 2AF

For your information:
This declaration enables the charity to reclaim 28p
from Inland Revenue for every £1.00 that you donate,
as long as you have paid income tax in the last year.
This costs you nothing, but means a lot to us.
Please notify us if your circumstances change and you
no longer pay tax. If you pay tax at the higher rate
you can continue claiming tax relief when completing
your tax return.

DATA PROTECTION ACT 1998 Members' data will be used by Friends of Oldway,
to collect the agreed Gift Aid tax relief from Inland Revenue.

www.saveoldway.com

THE CHILDREN COME OF AGE

Over the next few years the Wigwam stood empty, looked after by the Singer family's resident steward, Mr McCormack.

As the children grew up, various schemes were devised by the family lawyer Charles Eastley to protect their financial independence and individual fortunes from their new French step-father. Mortimer had already set up home at Redworth House in Totnes. Washington was the first to join him, followed by Paris and Franklin. Winnaretta and Belle Blanche had married into the French aristocracy and so would not follow their brothers back to Devon.

Washington had purchased Steartfield House on the seafront at Paignton (today's Palace Hotel) as his private residence. The Wigwam was still owned by Isaac's Trust; as such no one brother could make it his exclusive home. It was used for family celebrations though – and the largest of these was the month of festivities for Paris Singer's coming of age in November 1888. Only now, fifteen years after it was completed, did the Wigwam finally host the sort of grand entertainments Isaac had intended. A month of festivities saw masked balls for over 200 people, productions in the Wigwam's theatre featuring stars from the Grand Opera in

Paris, and grand firework displays in the gardens. Typical evenings would see the party move from the theatre in the Wigwam, through the great conservatory and into the Rotunda, which was transformed into a fabulously decorated ballroom. The less well-off were not forgotten either – balls for tradesmen were also hosted, and coupons were distributed to the poor of the town to buy provisions in local shops and so join in the celebrations.

As part of the festivities Paris Singer gave £2,000 to pay for a new organ to be placed in the Paignton Parish Church of St John.

Washington and Mortimer had previously given £2,000 to pay for the building of the Paignton Cottage Hospital.

Above Washington Singer.

PARIS SINGER RETURNS

After these great birthday celebrations were over, however, the sons would again move out, and the Wigwam was left empty once more. The family's love affair with Paignton meanwhile continued elsewhere.

In 1893 Paris Singer bought the Redcliffe Towers (today's hotel), intending to make that his principal Paignton residence. Washington Singer was installed in Steartfield, and Mortimer Singer had bought the adjoining Middlepark Villa in 1887, so the three brothers were now neighbours. A long-drawn-out legal case brought against the Trustees of Isaac's estate saw the Wigwam and all its grounds put up for auction in 1892, but the reserve price was not reached, and the house and grounds were withdrawn from the sale.

To come so close to losing their father's Wigwam was doubtless too much for two of the brothers. Washington stepped in and bought the Wigwam from the Singer Trustees in 1893 to safeguard it for the family. Paris Singer almost immediately took a half share in the house with his brother. Paris later took over his brother's share of the house and grounds, and finally moved in permanently in 1897. He immediately started on plans to make his

own improvements, to shape the house to his taste and needs. His father's Wigwam needed to be updated.

The first step was to engage the most famous landscape architects and garden designers of the time, the Frenchmen Achille and Henri Duchêne, to draw up a vision to transform his new home.

Above The Redcliffe Towers in 1893.

Right Paris Singer.

Opposite Mr and Mrs Mortimer and Paris Singer and their cars, 1902. A Panhard (left) and a Napier (right).

In 1897 the Duchênes produced a plan — a drawing of a new mansion house and gardens inspired by the Palace of Versailles. Like all Duchêne landscapes, it was to be a fusion of different elements; formal gardens, lawns and parterres, with woodland, lakes and a grotto. A new sloping bank was created to lead down to an area specially prepared for sports and tennis.

Prior to his first visit to Oldway in 1897, Achille Duchêne had been busy restoring the gardens and buildings of the Petit Trianon at the Palace of Versailles in France. Duchêne designed the new classical south front, inspired by the "Pavillon Français" in the gardens there. Paris Singer wasted no time in turning this vision into a reality. By 1900, the Paignton Observer reported, the new front was finished and clashed unacceptably with the original Victorian yellow brick house. Statues took pride of place on plinths at the end of the newly created formal south lawns. On a lower level an orangery was created next to a grotto with a waterfall cascading over it.

Opposite The original Duchene vision, 1897.

Above Left Henri Duchêne.

Below Left Achille Duchêne.

THE DUCHÊNE VISION MADE REALITY

The new Duchêne gardens had sunken lawns with a broad central avenue leading to the centre of the south front. This wide path was put a strong emphasis on the centre bay of the front; an aspect of the design that is now lost to us. This feature was removed in the 1920s to create a tennis court for the Country Club. An avenue of pleached limes that runs the length of the boundary with Little Oldway survives today, again inspired by the gardens of the Petit Trianon. Orange trees in tubs lined the paths in the summer and over-wintered in the orangery by the grotto.

Paris Singer made exact copies of statues in the gardens at Versailles to ornament the grounds at Oldway, and plinths were provided to display these.

Photography was a important part of the Duchênes' way of working, and they photographed their projects at different stages of completion.

Below The centre bay of the south front was aligned on the Duchêne's central avenue through the lawns.

Above The south front was completed in 1900, with the work on the gardens underway.

In the garden of the Petit Trianon at Versailles, the "Pavillon Français" was designed by Ange-Jacques Gabriel in 1750 as a place for relaxation and dining, used by Marie Antoinette for balls and concerts. The inspiration for the corner pavilions and the style of the new south front by Duchêne can be clearly seen here.

Duchêne carefully recreated each element of the garden of the Petit Trianon at Oldway – sphinxes, urns, statues, pine trees and orangery, even lakes with rocky outcrops and a grotto.

Opposite The Pavillion Francais, in the Petit Trianon gardens at Versailles.

Above Sphinxes and orangery in the Petit Trianon gardens, both recreated at Oldway.

In Isaac's time the approach to the house had always been along a drive running around the outside perimeter of the estate, eventually approaching the house from the west (the side Little Oldway is today).

Paris's new house would use the same route (the access road from the main Torquay Road was only put in around 1918). He created a full size replica of the Porte Saint Antoine from Versailles to act as a triumphal entrance to his courtyard. In Versailles the original similarly forms the entrance to the Trianon gardens from outside world.

The re-modelling to the house necessitated the removal around 1904 of the great conservatory that joined the Rotunda to the main house. The palms inside were given to the town to plant in the new Victoria Park.

Far left Porte Saint Antoine, Versailles.

Left The same recreated at Oldway.

Above The rock features and lake from the Petit Trianon were copied at Oldway.

Left This urn was the model for those reproduced at Oldway.

33

The next phase of Paris Singer's transformation saw modern construction techniques, steel girders and concrete, used to create a great classical colonnade, in the style of Place de la Concorde in Paris (home to the Automobile Club de France which he knew so well). The basement of the Wigwam, formerly storerooms and servants' quarters underground, was opened up to form a new ground floor level, and to compensate, a new range of servants' rooms were incorporated into the roof.

By 1904 all of the Duchêne landscaping, the flat sports hippodrome and tennis area, the sloping lawns and parterres were complete, with the grotto and lakes of the lower gardens still under construction.

Above Window detail, east front.

By 1910 the house as we know it today was completed. Paris Singer's grand design would remain incomplete, leaving the west front of the house untouched as a reminder of his father's creation. To emphasise the change, the Wigwam was renamed Oldway House, with Oldway Villa becoming Little Oldway as we know it today.

Opposite left The construction of the east front's colonnade.

Opposite right Place de la Concorde, Paris.

Above A nearly completed Oldway, circa 1910.

THE CROWNING OF JOSEPHINE

The inspiration for the entire rebuilding inside and out at Oldway was doubtless the creation of the grand staircase, with its centrepiece of David's painting "The Crowning of Josephine by Napoleon".

Paris Singer had bought the painting at auction in 1898 following a visit from the Duchênes earlier in the month. Paris went to great lengths to be true to the original Versailles staircase. He was creating a design here worthy of royalty at its most powerful, and through his French mother he saw the link with Louis XIV as quite appropriate.

The creation of the staircase and new ballroom required the removal of Isaac's beloved theatre, but otherwise the majority of the house internally remained little changed by the alterations. The approach to the staircase was made through the entrance we use today. In the days of the Wigwam this entire floor we pass through to get to the staircase had been servants' quarters and rooms for storage.

Right The grand staircase at Oldway.

Above Trophy: the weapons of Hercules.

Right The Ambassadors' staircase, engraving by Louis Surugue de Surgis (1686-1762).

Vuë du costé gauche
du grand Escalier de Versailles.

Prospectus partis sinistra
majorum Scalarum Versalianarum.

J.M. Chevotet del.

Surugue excud.

THE AMBASSADORS' STAIRCASE

The Ambassador's Staircase at Versailles was so called because it was here that foreign representatives were made to wait before being able to address King Louis XIV. It was designed by Charles Le Brun and François d'Orbay in 1672, and quickly became one of the architectural wonders of Europe. A double staircase was relatively rare at this time, and one lit by daylight through a great internal roof lantern was equally impressive to contemporaries. Sadly the staircase was demolished by Louis XIV to create an apartment for his daughter Madame Adelaide in the Palace.

At Oldway with the exception that the design of the original is adapted to accommodate the great painting of "The Crowning of Josephine", nearly all the other details in the marble floors and other decoration are faithfully reproduced.

There exists today only one other reproduction of this staircase in the world, built by King Ludwig II of Bavaria at the Royal Palace of Herrenchiemsee as a "Bavarian Versailles" in 1878.

Above The marble floors at Oldway - Paris Singer sourced the marble from the same quarries used by Louis XIV, and imported Italian marble specialists to cut it.

Left The Ambassadors' staircase, engraving by Louis Surugue de Surgis (1686-1762).

THE PAINTED CEILING

The original ceiling was painted by Charles le Brun. Le Brun was officially the "First Painter to his Majesty Louis XIV", and worked extensively in Versailles, notably in the Hall of Mirrors.

Since the role of the Staircase was to create a sense of awe in the waiting ambassadors, he brought the entire known world to this ceiling, and with it depictions of all the foreign policy triumphs of Louis's reign.

The four continents; America, Europe, Africa and Asia are all depicted by the four ships' prows, one in each corner. The classical Muses are depicted seated in the centre of each panel representing painting, architecture, tragedy, astronomy, history, music and poetry. Paris Singer's artists had permission from the French government to erect scaffolding in Versailles to study intricately the techniques and colours Le Brun used.

Above ceiling detail - the four ships' prows symbolise the four continents known to Louis XIV's time.

Right The magnificent painted ceiling at Oldway.

CONSTRUCTING THE GARDENS

Whilst the interior was being refashioned, work went on outside to bring the Duchêne designs to fruition. Isaac's gardens had been mostly gentle lawns lined with woodland, but now an entirely new designed landscape was being created. The renowned garden designer F. W. Meyer oversaw the creation of the grotto, lakes and pine tree areas, along with an adjoining tropical garden planted with palms.

Opposite At work in the lower garden.

Above left The newly finished grotto.

Left *The construction of the ponds and tropical gardens.*

THE ROTUNDA – FROM STABLES TO SWIMING POOL

Isaac Singer loved horses, and had a range of special carriages built throughout his lifetime. Whilst in New York he had even designed and had built a canary yellow "sociable" – a carriage that could accommodate thirty-one passengers, and which was drawn by a team of nine matched horses.

By the time he got to Paignton his ambitions were more modest - the largest he had here could hold eighteen passengers – and this along with his other bespoke carriages was stored in the outer ring of the Rotunda. His coaches were ordered from Messrs. Edwards Coachbuilders of Torquay, who would exhibit their newly made models for people to come and see.

That age had passed, however, and Paris and Lillie Singer were determined to make their mark on the Rotunda as well. The central exercising area was altered to construct an oblong swimming pool tiled in blue with white marble edges. The horse stalls that had been in the second part of the building's outer ring were now replaced with changing rooms. The swimming pool survives to this day under the floor, and was used continuously up the end of the Second World War.

Below left Paris Singer's swimming pool survives under the floor of the Rotunda.

Below right The Rotunda seen from Southfield Avenue.

ISADORA DUNCAN

Paris Singer had started an affair with the famous dancer Isadora Duncan in 1909, and had soon become captivated by her. In May 1910 Isadora gave birth to their child, Patrick, and Paris invited Isadora to stay in his newly completed Oldway in September of that year. This was to be a trial marriage, which Paris hoped would convince Isadora to accept a more permanent arrangement.

Paris gave her numerous staff to look after her every whim, a yacht in the Bay and glamorous motor cars at her disposal.

Life in England was not to her liking however – she complained of the constant rain in Devon, and a lifestyle that was centred around eating endless meals with countless courses. Life as Paris Singer's second wife was not for her, and that decision was the start of a long and painful period of separation. Both her children were to die shortly afterwards in a terrible car accident, drowning in the River Seine in Paris in April 1913. She herself would also die in a car accident of sorts – strangled in September 1927 by the length of her flowing scarf which caught around the wheel of a car she was being driven in.

The twentieth century brought drastic changes to the life Paris Singer had known and enjoyed. The difficult relationship with Isadora and separation from his first wife Lillie kept Paris increasingly away from Paignton. (They would finally divorce in 1918 on the grounds of his misconduct.) His health worsened with a suspected stroke in 1910. All these factors, combined with increasingly large income tax bills, meant that by the outbreak of the First World War in 1914 Oldway was not to be a family home for much longer.

Above Isadora Duncan as the first fairy in "Midsummer Night's Dream".

At the outbreak of the First World War Paris Singer paid for Oldway to be converted into the American Women's War Hospital. The hospital was a way American ladies living in the UK could contribute to the war effort, and give something back to Britain at a time of great need.

The photographs taken during its time as a hospital show the house and the Duchene garden at their peak, having been completed only a short time previously.
All of Oldway was given over to the war effort. The Banqueting Hall became Mary Ward, and the Rotunda St George Ward. Even the grand reception rooms and ballroom were converted to take patients.

The upstairs rooms were also used by the hospital. Once stately bedrooms now housed ten to twelve patients. There was an operating theatre at the top of the main staircase, an X-ray room, a dispensary and an isolation ward. Nurses lodged in the servants' rooms in the roof, or else in the adjoining villas of Fernham or Little Oldway. The great painting on the staircase was removed for safekeeping by Paris Singer to his house in New York, to be returned when the war was over.

Above Staff of Paget Ward, Christmas 1914.

Right The new ballroom became Alexandra Ward with beds for 30 patients.

This was not the first time the Singers had helped out in times of national crisis. Paris's Redcliffe Towers was donated as a hospital for the Boer War, fitted out at his brother Washington's expense, with beds sponsored by the rich, as was the practice here at Oldway now. Both Mortimer and Washington also gave their principal residences to be converted to hospitals.

Over 5,000 casualties were treated at Oldway (with only 19 deaths) before it was taken over as a military hospital and run by the American Red Cross in 1918 (as were the Redcliffe and the Esplanade Hotels on Paignton seafront).

In the words of one patient:

> "The Hospital was a heaven for wounded men. They were allowed every privilege possible conducive with the rules and military discipline."

Americans only arrived in numbers from 1918 when the hospital was taken over by the American Red Cross; until then only British and Colonial soldiers had been sent there.

Paris Singer and the hospital were deeply honoured by the visit in November 1914 of Queen Mary – the first visit to any hospital outside of London by either the King or his consort.

Below Nurses and patients pose in front of one of the statues painstakingly copied from Versailles.

Paris Singer himself had been one of those present at Paignton train station to meet the first load of wounded bound for Oldway in 1914.

His only daughter Winnaretta decided to work at the hospital, starting at the very bottom and working her way up to the rank of Sister. She was finally forced to leave her post there as the result of an infection.

Whilst the number of fatalities had been small up to 1918, the time of the American Red Cross would see heavy loss of life resulting from the global flu pandemic as it spread across Europe. "Terrible death toll at Oldway" was the headline of the Paignton Observer on 10 October 1918.

The hospital finally closed at the end of February 1919, after four and a half years. The equipment was given to Paignton Hospital for the good of the town.

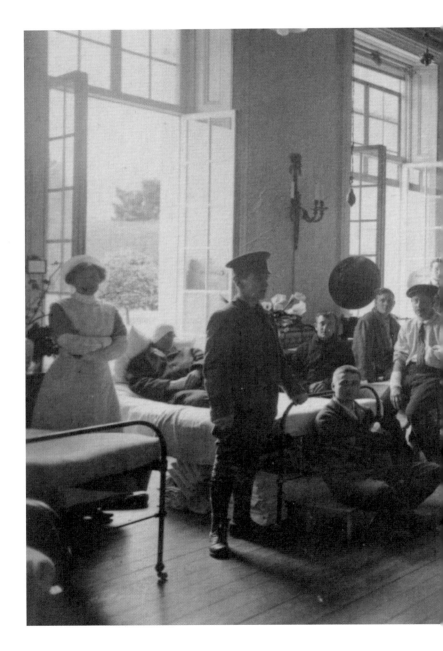

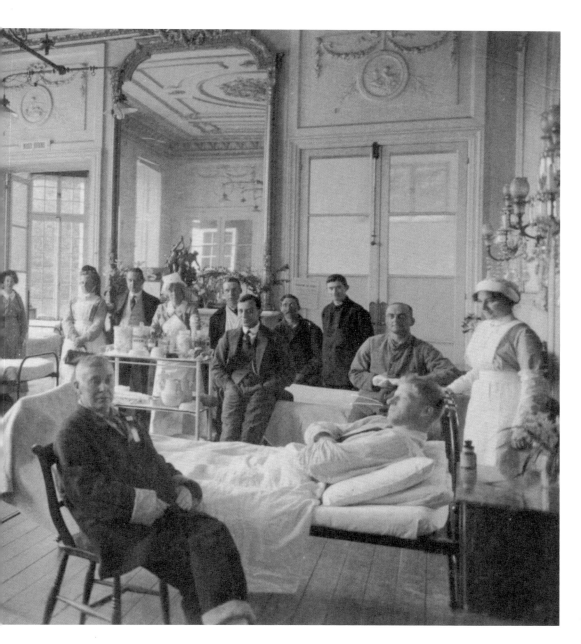

Left The former billiard room became Churchill Ward.

THE TORBAY COUNTRY CLUB

By the end of the First World War Paris Singer had moved on from Oldway to new projects in France and America. His wife Lillie was to remain in Paignton until her death in 1951, living in a house built by Paris on the newly created Marine Drive in Preston. Mortimer and Washington would also remain in England until their deaths, maintaining close links with Paignton and its institutions.

Oldway House was now closed up, and it, together with the rest of Paris Singer's land, had been transferred into the ownership of the Paignton and District Land Development Company, in all some 500 acres in and around the town were managed by it. A new role for the estate had yet to be decided upon.

It was 1923 before a new use was found. The Redcliffe Gymkhana sports and tennis club, opposite the Redcliffe Hotel on Paignton seafront, was in need of a new home as the land along the new Marine Drive into Preston was to be developed. The club accepted the Singer Estate's invitation to transfer its base to Oldway. The place seemed perfectly suited for this new role: the land at the foot of the slope in front of the grand colonnade had been landscaped by the Duchênes for tennis originally. Paris Singer had already converted the Rotunda from a riding school into a grand swimming bath in the 1890s, and with badminton added as a facility in the banqueting hall the Torbay Country Club was born, with Paris Singer as its President.

The Country Club was a successful, exclusive organization welcomed and frequented by Paignton's wealthy. The villa of Little Oldway served as club house and bridge club, but the great house itself still remained empty. In late 1929, new plans were unveiled. The Club was to be expanded. Bowls would be introduced with the creation of two rinks of the highest-quality Cumberland turf. Squash courts would be built at the rear of the Rotunda. More tennis courts would be laid. There was talk of a golf course, and of converting the main house into a residential wing of the Club. Grand plans were proposed: a hundred bedrooms with as many bathrooms available for members to rent. This expansion would necessitate a widening, and democratization, of the membership base. Paris Singer wanted members to be accepted on the basis of how good a citizen or sportsman they were, rather than on the basis of their wealth or connections. It was planned to recruit amongst the professional classes in the cities; lawyers and doctors would travel down for short breaks and stay in the house's newly converted accommodation.

Opposite top The newly built bowling greens.

Opposite bottom Aerial view of the Country Club, circa 1934.

Left *Lawn tennis at the Country Club.*

Above Members relaxing in the colonnade.

By the mid 1930s the Torbay Country Club was Paignton's greatest asset. The introduction of bowling was a big success, and time after time visiting teams sang the praises of what they described as "a bowling-centre unequalled in Devon and throughout the country". The role the great house was to play in this new success was, however, still undecided. The hundred-bedroom residential club had not materialized. Little by little the Country Club took over use of the grand first floor rooms, whilst the upstairs floors were modified to form seven residential apartments, of which the Singer family held at least one.

The death of Paris Singer in June 1932 was reported with great sadness in the local newspapers. Paris's final years saw his attention shift to the development of a new project, the laying out of Palm Beach,

Florida and the Everglades Club, with the help of the architect Addison Mizner. In his absence Washington and Mortimer had continued to fund local good causes such as Paignton Hospital and Paignton Parish Church, as well as the emerging University of the South West at Exeter to which Washington gifted £25,000.

In September 1932 the final, long-awaited, stage of the development of the Country Club was announced. An eighteen hole golf course, designed by the Ryder cup professional James Braid, would be built on land the Estate owned between Oldway and Marldon, creating the Torbay Golf and Country Club. Little Oldway was to be the Club House, and golfers would get to the first hole by a private road (today's Westhill Road). The course would extend up to the old windmill at the top of Marldon Road, giving the fairways stunning views over the Bay and of Dartmoor behind.

Select houses would be built for those wishing to live a short walk from the fairways. It was not long before members judged Little Oldway to be too far to walk for the nineteenth hole, and an impressive new club house was opened off the eighteenth green in May 1935.

Top The Club house of the golf course opened May 1935.

Opposite Winnaretta Singer as debutante.

52

A FAMILY HOME AGAIN

Throughout the period that Oldway was developing as a Country Club, one part would remain a family home for the Singers. One of the flats inside the mansion was reserved for family use, and this was home to Paris's daughter Winnaretta, and her family.

Winnaretta had married Sir Reginald Leeds, eldest son of Baron Leeds, and became Lady Leeds. She recalled in later life how theirs had been a case of love at first sight at a house party in Scotland attended by members of the royal family. She also recalled the dances and swimming parties her parents had held in the Rotunda, and her learning to swim by being dangled into the pool on the end of a pole at the age of three.

Together the couple would dominate local society throughout their lifetimes. The pictures from the Singer family album featured here show their life relaxing and growing up at Oldway in the 1930s and beyond. Their children, Rhodanthe and George, would be the last descendants of the Singer family to grow up at Oldway.

After a time living in the Mansion proper, the family moved into Little Oldway next door.

Above Relaxing in the gardens.

Above Right Sir Reginald and Lady Leeds.

Right Rhodanthe and George Leeds.

International events would intervene in Oldway's history once again before the end of the decade. In World War II Oldway was requisitioned by the RAF to serve Initial Training Wing (ITW) no. 4. The Country Club was used for eight lecture rooms, whilst on the seafront the Hydro, Ramleh, Esplanade and Palace hotels were also requisitioned. Oldway was attacked twice, once on 4 September 1942, when "extensive exterior damage" was caused by bombing and machine gunning, and once with incendiary and high-explosive bombs on 13 February 1943, when little damage was caused. Neither attack caused any casualties, and ITW 4 was wound up on 7 March 1944. The golf section of the Country Club managed to continue throughout the War, a measure of how independent it was now of the main house.

As the War drew to a close, the Directors of the Country Club decided that it would not re-open in its previous form when peace came. It had, the then President Captain Eastley said in a speech, never truly been financially viable, and it was only thanks to the generosity of the Singer Estate that it had been able to continue this long. The cost of the bowling rinks alone had been over £6,000, and the annual subscriptions received had hardly been able to cover the costs associated with that one part of the operation.

At the same time Paignton Urban District Council was looking for new premises – one large building where all their offices could relocate to, instead of being spread across several buildings in the town. There were two possibilities. The first was the Esplanade Hotel on the seafront (today's Inn on the Green). This had land extending from the rear of the building to the railway line giving ample space for building development to house the Council's staff. The second option was Oldway. An attempt to purchase from the Singer Estate had been made initially by the Council in 1924 when the building lay empty after its time as a hospital, but the asking price (£24,000) proved too high. This time the asking price was to be £46,000, with an option to buy the David painting on the staircase.

Above Initial Training Wing syllabus.

Above Oldway at sunrise.

Opposite The opening of Oldway as reported in the Paignton News, December 1946.

After much negotiation and secrecy, the Council opted for Oldway. The Singer Estate had given the Council first refusal to help in achieving the Singer family's wish that it should pass to the town if they were to sell it.

Oldway was bought with a loan from the Ministry of Health. A public inquiry was held to hear the case for granting the Council the fifty year loan to purchase it.

The principal argument for its purchase made by the Council was the public health benefit its sports facilities would bring to Paignton. It boasted tennis courts, a badminton court, a gymnasium, a swimming pool, two squash courts and croquet lawns. This would, the Council said, be a "green lung" for Paignton, "one of which it was in great need of already" Councillors at the time remarked. No-one at the inquiry spoke in opposition, and the loan was granted.

"...the acquisition of Oldway and grounds at a cost of £45,000 was one of the finest bits of work the Council has ever done. It was an absolute gift and the town had every right for being grateful to the Singer family for giving them the opportunity of acquiring it. We wanted to prevent anyone going there and building and spoiling the district."

Councillor Stabb, Chairman
Paignton Urban District Council,
1947

The official handover ceremony took place in December 1946, at a ball and dinner at which Lady Leeds gave a speech. She spoke of her father's wish to see Oldway as a Civic Centre, and how the family didn't feel they were losing Oldway; as inhabitants of Paignton they would all still have a share of it. There was an air of public excitement regarding the acquisition: "few people" the local paper remarked "will have seen inside the grand club house of the Torbay Country Club".

At this event she also announced that the French government were in negotiations

The "miniature Versailles"

The scene at the official opening of Oldway on Wednesday. Lady Leeds revealed that the picture, in the background, of the crowning of the Empress Josephine, painted for Napoleon by David, is in process of being acquired by the French Government, and will hang in the Palace of Versailles, in the place originally appointed for it, which up to now has remained vacant. She described Oldway as "the miniature Versailles."

CHURSTON W.I.

A satisfactory report on the past year was given at the annual meeting of Churston and Galmpton Women's Institute at the Congregational Schoolroom. Miss S. Lassam presided. An interesting talk on Dartmoor was given by Mrs. Howard, and Mrs. Richards was tea hostess.

Officers elected were: President, Miss Lassam; vice-presidents, Miss Braddon and Mrs. Paylor; hon. treasurer, Mrs. Holloway; and hon. secretary, Mrs. Sever.

Lady Leeds tells Oldway audience:

My father visualised this as civic centre

OFFICIALLY opening Paignton's new municipal buildings at Oldway, formerly the Singer family mansion, on Wednesday, Lady Leeds, daughter of Mr. Paris Singer and granddaughter of the late Mr. Isaac Merritt Singer, remarked:

"I am the only person I know who has been able to disprove the old adage about not being able to eat your cake and have it—for I still own Oldway jointly with my fellow Paigntonians."

Lady Leeds, who said she was proud of the honour conferred upon her, but confessed that her feelings were "rather mixed," also remarked: "When I realise that for more than 30 years Oldway has been given, in one way or another, to the service of the public, this new step is not such a drastic one as would at first appear, and in any case I know it is one of which my father would approve most profoundly. He always had the interests of Paignton most truly at heart, and always visualised this building as the eventual civic centre of Paignton.

PREVIOUS OFFER

"He offered it as such many years ago. It did not happen then, but it has happened now, and I can speak for my brothers as well as myself and say how very glad

with the Singer family for the return of the David painting.

The Council had decided not to buy the David painting. Instead, it was sold to the French government, who returned it to the Coronation Room of the Palace of Versailles in April 1947, where it still hangs today. A special railway carriage from France was brought over to transport it, with staff from the French Embassy attending to supervise the process.

When Paignton Council bought Oldway from the Singer Estate in 1946, the gardens had become neglected and overgrown. It took a team of gardeners five years to bring things back to how they had looked at the time of Paris Singer.

When the Council took possession of the Estate there were still tenants with leases for some of the seven apartments within the mansion house and Rotunda. As each lease finished the Council converted the space into offices – with the last tenant only vacating in December 1949. An arrangement was made with Lady Leeds for her family to continue to live at Little Oldway during her lifetime. Oldway was to remain in part a family home until then.

Top The removal of the painting by French officials.

Bottom The painting packed and ready for dispatch.

A NEW LEASE OF LIFE

Oldway from the start of Council ownership became a focal point for the town, hosting night after night of dancing and celebration. The annual Chairman's ball was regularly attended by over 300 guests.

People came from far and wide to see what was regarded by all as "the greatest civic centre in the Westcountry". One day in 1952 saw 1,400 visitors come up from Plymouth in thirty-eight coaches to visit the house and gardens. The Paignton Lawn Tennis Tournament the same year had over 150 entrants.

Events in the gardens were equally popular – in 1960 the English Folk Society brought in 400 children from all over Devon to dance on the south lawn.

It was under the Paignton Urban District Council's ownership that the house first became widely referred to as Oldway Mansion.

Above 400 children dance on the lawn, 1946.

Left Paris Singer's study becomes the council chamber.

FINDING A USE FOR THE ROTUNDA

From the start of Council ownership it was difficult to find a use for the Rotunda and its outbuildings. Initially the Council used the stable block for much needed storage for equipment taken off the beaches after the summer.

In late 1948 the Council was presented with an incredible offer: a new company, Oldway Film Studios, would rent the Rotunda and connected buildings for the sum of £3,500 per year. The Rotunda would be sound -proofed and converted to three film stages, with a view to making ten films each year. The venture was to be part of a government-backed drive to create a thriving independent film industry. There were seen to be great advantages of cost as well as location in being based in Paignton. Paignton would be Britain's Hollywood. Sadly a slump in the film industry meant the project hardly got off the ground. Within a year £2,000 of the rent was in arrears, and the company was largely paying its way with "improvements" to the Rotunda (including the removal of Isaac's cast iron balconies) in lieu of rent. The situation did not improve and in the summer of 1951 the film company's property was auctioned off.

Less than a year later, in May 1952, the Council unanimously approved a light industrial use of the Rotunda and Badminton Hall by Standard Telephones and Cables (STC), at a lower rent of £1,500 per annum. STC wanted a training and research facility whilst plans for their factory on Long Road, Paignton, were drawn up, this time the Council would not be disappointed by their tenants, who would stay on for more than twenty-five years in their "temporary" accommodation at Oldway.

Above The Rotunda in 2009.

50399. Oldway Mansion (Civic Centre), Paignton.

Little in the gardens has changed since 1946, with the notable exception of the Orangery which was demolished in 1958. This sadly had never recovered from damage sustained during the Second World War.

It had stood at the end of the terrace next to the Grotto and waterfall, and when demolished was replaced by a rockery and steps leading up to the wooded area and terrace from the lower level.

Left The Orangery in its prime circa 1930.

Above Oldway seen form the glass prism roof of the Orangery.

RECENT YEARS

The golf section of the Torbay Country Club would continue until 1955, when the land the golf course was on was developed for housing. A quarter of the adult population of Paignton – 4,294 people – signed a petition to stop the development and this was sent to Whitehall. Planning consent for building had, however, been granted in 1946 and the closure of the course and development could not be halted.

The Country Club survives in the thriving outdoor and indoor bowls presence in Oldway gardens. Tennis is still a major part of life in the grounds as it has been since the 1930s. Paignton Chess Congress held its first competition in the ballroom in 1951; 2010 marked its 60th birthday in the same location.

Lady Leeds would live on in Little Oldway until her death in January 1980, confined to her bed for her last years because of a spinal injury. She passed away in the same bedroom that Isaac had died in over a hundred years before.

Oldway was used as film location for part of the setting of the 1968 film Isadora starring Vanessa Redgrave. It has been used as a location in several other film and television productions since then.

An ambitious plan to turn the Rotunda and outbuildings into a vibrant theatre centre was launched in 1994, but sadly was unsuccessful.

Oldway has for some time been home to the Torbay Registry Office and is one of the most popular places for civil wedding ceremonies in England.

The Scanachrome copy of the original David painting was installed in 1995, thanks to the efforts of the Torbay Civic Society and assistance in particular from the Singer-Polignac foundation in Paris and Mrs Selous.

Torbay Council announced the decision to seek a partner developer to take on and restore Oldway at the end of 2006. The Friends of Oldway group was formed in February 2007 as a response to this decision.

The Mansion House is protected as a Grade II* building and the Rotunda and adjoining buildings are listed as Grade II. The gardens are listed Grade II on the National Register of Historic Parks and Gardens.

Left Paris Singer's
ballroom today

UNDERSTANDING OLDWAY

Oldway can be a shock to the senses when you approach it for the first time. In a land used to understated elegance, the sheer force and presence of the colonnaded East front is overwhelming. It seems completely out of place with its surroundings, concealed within the seaside town of Paignton. To appreciate it fully requires an understanding of the personalities of the men it was built for.

The original brick built mansion represented the triumph of Isaac Singer's vision of his dream home. The site – exactly one hundred feet about sea level, was specifically chosen so the building would dominate all it surveyed, a constant reminder of the presence, might and benevolence of its creator. Contemporary photos show how the Wigwam loomed over the small town of Paignton. It was unquestionably the product of the mind of Isaac Singer, and was the physical expression of his independent personality. It was a reflection of the great man, of his power and, at the same time, its name, the Wigwam, showed he had no desire to be pompous. In an era of aristocrats, he was content to be the native American chief, and the local population loved him for that.

The Victorian mansion was so much the personification of the father that any child who took it on would have to remodel it considerably if the house were to reflect anyone else. As soon as Paris took control of the building the rebuilding started, driven in the first instance by the skill of the foremost landscape designers of their day, the Duchênes. It ceased to be a wigwam, and instead became Oldway House.

The Duchêne design created, in the new south front, a delicate and essentially feminine design. The Pavillon Français was a favourite Marie Antoinette; and at Oldway the playful, haughty air of the sphinxes that sit overlooking the lawns embody her influence.

Paris Singer, however, wanted to draw ultimately on a different side of Versailles, that which reflected the masculine, all powerful Louis XIV. The staircase he created at great expense was the ultimate symbol of masculinity. Here was the French king's most impressive statement, combined, in the painting as its centrepiece, with Napoleon's moment of triumph, where he himself crowns Josephine Empress of the French, in defiance of the Pope who can only sit by and observe.

Once the Duchênes departed Paris Singer took control, and used his architectural training to turn the East and North fronts into bombastic statements of power that no-one could mistake for feminine. The result is a building that has more in common with the mansions built by American millionaires in Newport Rhode Island than the English country house.

As the project progressed it seems events in his personal life drew Paris away from the building, the original plans to remodel all four sides and demolish his father's beloved Rotunda were put on hold in favour of other projects, and once the entrance front and arch were complete the building work stopped. Thanks to this Oldway retains its unique combination of the vision of two very determined men, father and son, with limitless resources. It represents a fusion of styles, and beyond that a fusion of wills. It is equally a fusion of classical style and modern techniques, where columns are recreated not in solid stone, but with steel "I" bars and concrete.

What Paris had created was also more than could ever be a family home. So began a century of civic service, first as war hospital, then country club then civic centre.

In exploring Oldway you are not just exploring a building, but rather peeling back the layers of the minds that made it – its value is not just architectural, but as much in the social history it represents – the heritage of the Singer family in Torbay.

ACKNOWLEDGEMENTS

I am indebted to all of the people who have taken Oldway into their hearts, and who, in the face of sometimes overwhelming odds, have struggled to preserve its unique history to be passed onto future generations.

Principal among these is the recognised Singer and Oldway expert, John Wilson. His studies of the building and of Paris Singer are invaluable. He was the inspiration for the replica of the painting on the staircase. His research also saw the elevation of the Mansion from simple grade II to grade II*, and the listing of the Duchene garden on the Register of Historic Parks and gardens. The increase in the statutory protection that this brings will be fundamental to saving Oldway for future generations.

Rhodanthe Selous has been a great source of original material and guidance, and her support of the Friends of Oldway group as patron is invaluable. Her permission to include many photos from the private Singer family albums is thoroughly appreciated.

My parents, Joan and Brian Hawthorne have spurred me on from the beginning in my mission to save Oldway, and the Devon School of English has, both in terms of time and financial support, made this work possible.

A non-exhaustive list of those I need to thank:

The staff of Torquay Reference Library; Mark Pool, Janet Cooper and Caroline Jones
The Hallkeepers at Oldway past and present, Peter Davey & his team.
Dr Michael Rhodes
Paul Hope
Dorothy Gordon Smith
Torbay Council, in particular Hal Bishop and Christopher Pancheri
The Committee and Membership of the Friends of Oldway
Mike Lyons (Initial design)
Graham Forsdyke - International Sewing Machine Collectors' Society
Matthew Clarke (Torbay Bookshop)
Robert Letcher
Josephine Brown & Frances Brown
Michel Duchêne, Association Henri et Achille Duchêne
Dorothy Atkinson
Michael Robinson
David Parrott
Jean Waldman, American Red Cross
Peter Warren

Designed by Charlotte Burden

PHOTO CREDITS

Every effort has been made by the author to seek permission for any images used. Colour photography by the author.

I am indebted to the following copyright holders for their permission to reproduce images in this book:

Page(s)	Image and source
4	Portrait of Isaac Singer by Edward Harrisson May -National Portrait Gallery, Smithsonian Institution
5	Singer Sewing Machine no. 1- National Science Museum, London
6	Portrait of Isabelle Singer and children – private collection
8, 9, 10, 14, 24, 28, 29, 35, 46, 47, 49, 52, 59	Torbay Library Services
9	Portrait of G S Bridgman - Bob Brewis, historian for Torbay Lodge 1358 meeting at Paignton Masonic Hall
12, 34, 52, 62	Torquay Museum
14	Private collection
20-21	Dorothy Gordon Smith
22	Portrait of Lillie Singer – private collection
23	Portrait of Washington Singer – Mr Michael Robinson
24-25	Private collection
26-27	Association Henri & Achille Duchêne
38-39	Réunion des Musées Nationaux Picture Library, Paris
42-43	West Country Studies Library
45	Dr Michael Rhodes
50	Devon Record Office
53, 54, 58	Private collection
55	RAF archive

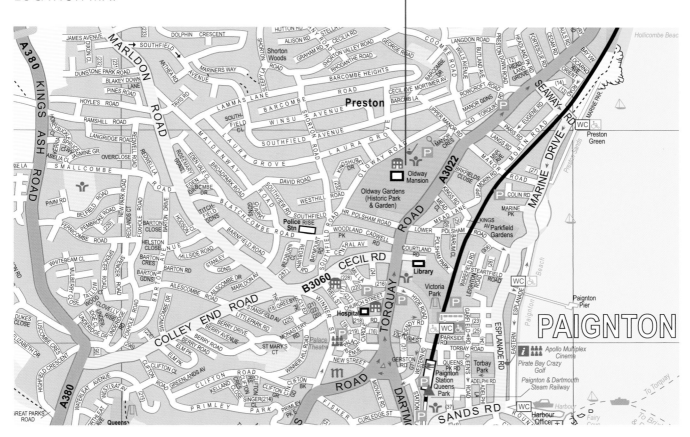

Kindly sponsored by

The Devon School of English
The Old Vicarage
1 Lower Polsham Road
Paignton Devon
TQ3 2AF ENGLAND

www.devonschool.co.uk
english@devonschool.co.uk

There is free public access to Oldway's gardens, and also to the public areas of the Mansion during office hours.